WELCOME TO THE WORLD OF ANIMALS

Bats

Diane Swanson

Gareth Stevens Publishing
A WORLD ALMANAC EDUCATION GROUP COMPANY

Please visit our web site at: **www.garethstevens.com**
For a free color catalog describing Gareth Stevens Publishing's list of high-quality books
and multimedia programs, call 1-800-542-2595 (USA) or 1-800-387-3178 (Canada).
Gareth Stevens Publishing's fax: (414) 332-3567.

The publishers acknowledge the support of the Canada Council for the Arts and the Cultural
Services Branch of the Government of British Columbia in making this publication possible.

The author acknowledges the experts at Bat Conservation International for reviewing this
manuscript.

Library of Congress Cataloging-in-Publication Data

Swanson, Diane, 1944-
   [Welcome to the world of bats]
  Bats / by Diane Swanson. — North American ed.
    p. cm. — (Welcome to the world of animals)
   Includes index.
   Summary: Describes the physical characteristics, behavior, habitat, and life cycle
of the only mammal with wings.
   ISBN 0-8368-3559-X (lib. bdg.)
   1. Bats—Juvenile literature. [1. Bats.] I. Title.
QL737.C5S92   2003
599.4—dc21   2002030279

This edition first published in 2003 by
Gareth Stevens Publishing
A World Almanac Education Group Company
330 West Olive Street, Suite 100
Milwaukee, WI 53212 USA

Series editor: Lauren Fox
Design: Katherine A. Goedheer
Cover design: Renee M. Bach

Cover photograph: Merlin D. Tuttle/Bat Conservation International
Photo credits: Merlin D. Tuttle/Bat Conservation International 4, 6, 8, 10, 12, 14, 16, 20, 22, 24,
26, 28, 30; Mark Kiser/Bat Conservation International 18

Printed in the United States of America

1 2 3 4 5 6 7 8 9 07 06 05 04 03

Contents

World of Difference

When darkness falls, bats rise to the skies. They are the only mammals that fly. Bats are furry and warm-blooded — like other mammals — but they also have wings. Thin skin stretched across the arms and fingers makes bat wings unique.

The legs of bats are just as special. Their knees point backward, making it easier for bats to perch, or roost. After a flight, they hover or somersault in midair, then land on their roosts — upside down.

Using sharp, curved claws, a bat hangs comfortably from one foot or two. Take-off is easy from that position. The bat just

A Townsend's big-eared bat dips down to a pond for a drink.

5

**For this hoary bat
tucked away in a tree,
it's time to rest.**

loosens its grip and spreads
its wings.

Small eyes buried in fur
fool many people into thinking
bats are blind. Actually, most
bats see well, and some have
excellent sight.

About one thousand
different kinds of bats fly the
world's skies. In North America
alone, there are more than forty

types of bats. Many weigh less than this book, and their wings spread a bit wider than this page. One of the biggest bats in North America, the hoary bat, has wings that can reach across two of these pages. On other continents, there are huge bats with wingspreads of more than 65 inches (165 centimeters).

Many bats are brown, but some are streaked with silver or trimmed with yellow "collars." One handsome kind of bat is black with three white spots on its back.

AMAZING BATS

Bats often surprise people. Here are some of the reasons why:

- **Each kind of bat makes its own special calls.**

- **Bats can swim, paddling with their wings. Many can also walk on their wrists — after they fold up their wings.**

- **The fossil of a bat that lived fifty million years ago looks a lot like today's bats.**

- **Thirsty bats lick drops of water that form on their coats in cool caves.**

Where in the World

Bats are everywhere — almost. The only continent without bats is Antarctica. In countries around the world, bats live in deserts, on grasslands, in forests — even in cities.

Some kinds of bats roost in trees. Their fur is thick enough to keep them warm outdoors and is colored to hide them. The red bat, for example, looks like a dying leaf, and the hoary bat looks like tree bark.

Other kinds of bats head indoors to roost. They hang inside caves, old mines, church towers, and attics. Some even roost in little wooden bat houses that people

This red bat hangs around in leafy trees, trying to hide from crows.

9

Townsend's big-eared bats roost inside shelters, such as this old winery.

build for them. Many bats have several roosts so they can rest between feedings.

Bats may use large openings to swoop into their resting spots, or they may squeeze through little cracks — some as narrow as a pencil.

Where the weather turns cold in autumn, many bats move to warmer places. Others stay put and hibernate — entering a deep winter sleep. Some other kinds do both — first migrating, then hibernating. Bats don't usually travel far, but some fly several hundred miles (kilometers) to winter homes. Silver-haired bats have even flown over ocean waters, stopping to rest on ships 150 miles (240 kilometers) out at sea.

At one time, there were many more bats than there are today. And more than twenty different kinds are in danger of disappearing from North America.

BAT MANSION

A crowd was touring a huge mansion, once the home of a multi-millionaire. Everything about the mansion was grand: the graceful ball-room, the fancy indoor and outdoor swimming pools, and the full-sized bowling alley.

One young girl on the tour stopped to admire the mansion's only resident. A little brown bat was snuggled between a double pane of glass in a door. After a day's sleep, it would zoom through the mansion and out into the night.

World on the Wing

What a fine flier the bat is. Moving each l-o-n-g finger that frames its wings, it can twist and circle about with ease. The skin between the tail and back legs of many bats also helps them fly. On both the tail and wings, the skin is rubbery. This skin does not tear easily, and it mends quickly. It is also free of hair, which would slow down a bat's flight.

The most nimble fliers are often the smaller, slower bats. They have short, broad wings that they can angle easily. Less nimble fliers usually have long, narrow wings meant for power and speed. Some of

Mexican free-tailed bats fly off to hunt. Millions may emerge from one cave.

13

When spotted bats fly, they hold their tall, pink ears straight up.

the swiftest, the red bats, can fly 40 miles (65 kilometers) an hour. Another fast flier, the Mexican free-tailed bat, has big ears set sideways so that they don't slow the bat down by catching air.

Bats might crash onto their noses if their necks weren't so short. The strong jaws and teeth of meat-eating bats make them heavy in front. Short necks help keep their weight centered. Being able to digest meals quickly also helps bats fly. It takes food only twenty minutes to pass through a little brown bat. (It takes food about twenty hours to pass through you.) As a result, bats don't have to carry around the extra weight for long.

When bats take a break from flying, they snuggle their hands and arms close to their bodies. Their wing skin folds like an umbrella, safely tucked away until the next time they take to the skies.

HEADING HOME

Like people, bats prefer living in their own homes. They often return to the same tree or cave, and they are good at finding their homes. Scientists took one big brown bat 250 miles (400 kilometers) from home, but it flew back on its own.

How bats find their way is a mystery. Sight seems to help some of them. They use bridges, buildings, and mountains to guide them. And they seem to teach their young how to find even tiny entrances to caves.

15

World of Words

Bats use sound for more than bat chat. Many make noise to pinpoint prey and find their way in the dark. Using their noses, mouths, or both, bats SQU-E-A-L very loudly. But the sounds are so high-pitched that people cannot hear them.

When the squeals strike an object, they bounce back — as echoes — to the bat's big ears. Then the bat's brain decodes the echoes. It can tell the size, shape, and texture of the object. The bat can also tell how far away the object is and — if the object is moving — which way it is heading and how fast it is going.

"I'm all ears," the California leaf-nosed bat seems to say. It hears very well.

All this information helps meat-eating bats chase prey and avoid smacking into rocks and trees. In fact, listening to echoes works so well that a bat can easily sense a tiny insect. As bats move into an area, they make hundreds of sounds to get the information they need.

Bats also listen to one another's high squeals for clues

Bat squeals help other bats find new roosts, such as this bat house.

about where to find prey and good places to roost. When they are just "talking," though, they often click and chirp low enough that humans can hear them. Young bats, or pups, call for their mothers, each pup using a different sound.

The most contented sounds do not come from the bat's mouth or nose. When a number of big brown bats roost together, their bodies may tremble gently. The movement makes a humming sound, called body buzz. As the bats fall asleep, the buzz slowly fades until all is quiet.

PALLID PRATTLE

Scientists observed several pallid bats to learn about their language. Here's what the bats seemed to be saying:

- "Hey, you. We're roosting over here. Join us." (Short, fast, loud calls from a group to one bat.)

- "You're annoying me." (Buzzing sound made with the teeth showing and the wings held out.)

- "Ah, this is peaceful." (A steady "chitter, chitter, chitter" by the whole group of bats.)

19

World Full of Food

Caterpillars crunching. Centipedes strolling. The softest sounds bring some bats rushing. Most North American bats eat about half their body weight in food each night. Mother bats nursing their young need twice that much.

A few bats in the United States and Mexico feed on fruit, nectar, and pollen, but most North American bats eat insects. Some also eat other prey, such as mice and lizards. Blood-feeding vampire bats live only in Mexico, Central America, and South America.

Using their echoes to find prey, most insect-eating bats hunt and feed in the air.

The lesser long-nosed bat feeds on nectar and pollen in cactus flowers.

21

A pallid bat crawls after a scorpion, then attacks. What a yummy meal!

Although they may have to dive and flip around to nab an insect, they are very good at it. A little brown bat can snap up hundreds of mosquitoes in one hour.

As most bats hunt, their wings scoop insects toward their open mouths. Many kinds of bats also use their tail skin as insect scoops.

Bats hunt close to home or travel a long way to their hunting spots. Mexican free-tailed bats may fly 60 miles (95 kilometers) each night, sometimes riding strong winds and rising high in the sky. Red bats may just head for bright lights, which attract swarms of insects.

Some bats hunt prey on plants or on the ground. The pallid bat pounces on spiders, scorpions, and insects. Then it usually returns to its roost to dine. Like other bats, it has thumb claws that are useful for handling its catch.

A Hunter That Really Clicks

Just after sunset, a spotted bat swoops down from its roost. On its menu are moths that can hear the high-pitched squeals many bats make. It's a good thing spotted bats hunt with lower clicks that these moths cannot hear.

Soon the bat snaps up a moth, removes its wings, legs, and antennae, and gobbles up the rest. The bat attacks every forty-five seconds, eating while it flies. The hunt lasts for five or six hours before the bat heads home.

Sleepy World

Bats may nap at night and sleep all day, but most need even more rest than that. They burn a lot of energy just keeping their body temperature normal. When it's cold outside, or if they can't catch much food, bats may save energy by sleeping deeply for hours — or even months. Sleeps that last all winter are called hibernation.

When a bat sleeps deeply, its body temperature falls close to air temperature. Its breathing may drop from about 200 to 25 breaths per minute, and its heart slows, too. The heartbeat of a little brown bat can fall from 200 to only 5 beats per minute.

Drowsy little brown bats cling to the ceiling of a damp cave.

25

For deep sleeps, most bats need shelter that is quiet, cool, damp, dark, and safe from enemies, such as owls, hawks, and raccoons. For many bats, that shelter might be a cave or an unused mine. Where winters are mild, it might be a hollow tree or a crack in a rock. But the red bat can hibernate while hanging from a branch, even in cold weather. It just curls up into a furry ball.

Snuggled together, these gray bats are sleeping the winter away.

Once bats have found a good spot to hibernate, they may use it for years. Males and females often crowd together. In one cave, 150 Indiana bats roost in an area about the size of this page.

Many kinds of bats build up fat to live on while they hibernate. When the weather warms up, a bat's heart starts beating faster. Its breathing speeds up, and its temperature rises. About twenty minutes later, it wakes up. Yawning, stretching, wriggling, it's ready to fly again.

BEAUTY AND THE BAT

Besides getting their beauty sleep, bats spend at least an hour a day washing. They clean themselves with their tongues, wetting their thumbs to wash their heads. Twisting about, they can lick both sides of their wings and tail.

Bats also comb their coats. Most use the claws on their feet, licking the dirt off between combings. Some bats comb with their bottom teeth. But whatever they use, bats keep themselves handsome and clean.

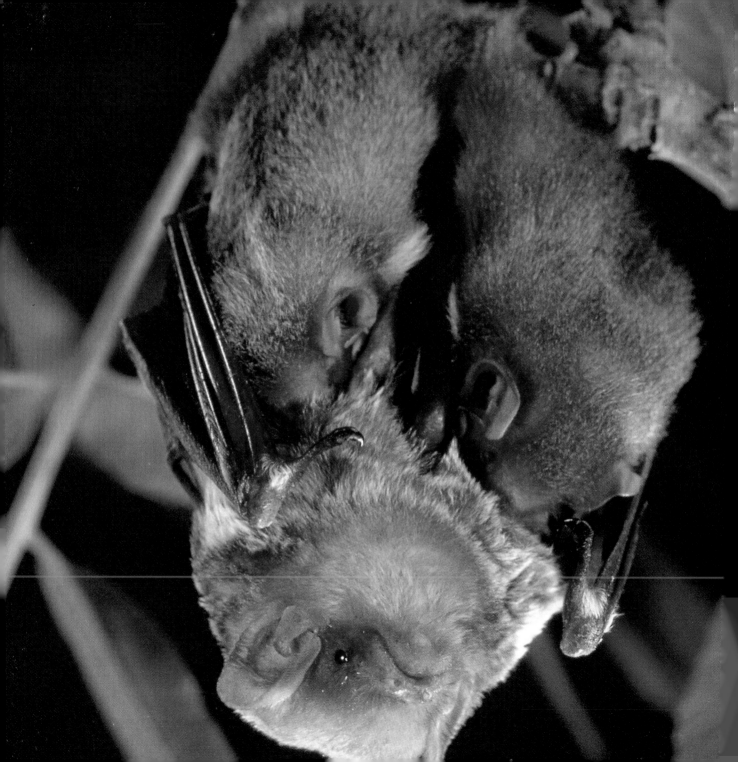

# New World

Most bats start life in a crowd. After hibernating, many females form huge nurseries — often in caves or old mines. They usually give birth to one pup each in spring or summer. But tree bats, such as hoary bats, may have up to four pups.

A bat enters the world back end first. Then its mother licks it clean. The pup clings to her fur, grips a nipple with its tiny, hooked teeth, and drinks her milk.

The pup usually weighs about one-fourth as much as its mother and grows fast. In a few days, it opens its eyes and perks up its ears. Dark fur starts to cover its naked body.

This red bat is a busy mother. She has two pups to feed.

29

Mother yuma bats listen and sniff to find their own pups in this attic nursery.

When the mother hunts, she leaves her new pup behind. A few female bats may baby-sit. If a pup falls off its roost, a baby-sitter carries it back.

After a few days, some pups start to play while their mothers are away. They romp around, crawling over each other and pretending to bite.

Most pups practice flying inside the nursery. They fall, then start flapping their wings. The hardest part of flying in a nursery is not bumping into other student fliers.

Soon a pup starts to follow its mother when she hunts. It listens and watches to learn how to find food. If it gets lost, it squeaks for its mother.

When they are about three months old, most pups can look after themselves. If they're lucky, they might live for years. Little brown bats may live to age thirty.

THE BATS CAME BACK

A spring fire destroyed an old, deserted church where about two thousand yuma bats gave birth and raised their pups each year. Luckily, no bats burned in the fire, but they all had to find a new nursery.

Several hundred of the bats moved into the warm attic of a general store. Others settled into wooden bat houses that people had built especially for them. The town was thrilled: its yuma bats were back!

Glossary

decodes — translates a signal so it can be understood.

digest — to change food in the stomach and intestines so it can be used by the body.

fossils — remains or traces of animals or plants that have been left in rock.

hibernate — to spend the winter in a deep sleep.

mammals — warm-blooded animals with backbones, some hair, and the ability to produce milk to feed their young.

migrating — moving from one region or climate area to another for a season.

nectar — a sweet liquid produced by flowers.

nursing — providing milk to a baby.

prey — animals that are hunted by other animals for food.

pups — the babies or young of bats and some other animals.

roost — (n) the place where a bat or bird rests.

Index